MW01127722

ISBN: 978-1-7343389-0-4

ACKNOWLEDGEMENTS

To the readers, I pray this book serves as a toolbox to those of you who are trying to survive the trivial obstacles most of us experience through life. To my children, thanks for the sacrifice of your childhood as my classroom. You could never learn more from me in our short lives together than I learned from you, but I pray I leave the lasting love and impact that you have on me, on you. For my friends who pushed, pulled, and dealt with the many discussions about this book, thank you for your ear, hearts, and minds. To my love, I love you. You did the real work: suffering me through it all. To my mentors, honestly, that was the birth of Necessary Confinement - the realization that I cannot be better with everyone having access and input. It is all about choosing the right people. That's what you have all been.

FOREWORD

Many of you will gain an insurmountable amount of value and understanding from reading the chapters within Necessary Confinement. I am delighted to write this foreword not only because I am devoted to the process of self-development but because I have firsthand experience from employing the principles revealed within the chapters of this book.

Wes assisted me significantly on my development journey. It is through him that I understand the need for mental confinement, DIET (Discipline In Every-Thing), and WORK (We Overcome with Real Knowledge). They are necessary components I apply to any goal I wish to achieve.

Two years ago, I was challenged to complete one half and one full marathon. I thought the challenge was out of reach because running sucks but accepted nonetheless. This would be the first time I applied DIET and WORK, and they both worked. I achieved success and completed the full and half marathon by having faith, committing to the task mentally, being disciplined, and doing the work; all things fervently expressed in this book. Since then, I have completed an additional ten (10) half marathons and plan to complete more. I attest, applying the principles and practices within Necessary Confinement will bring you success. I must warn you; these principles and practices require a lifestyle change. The work is continuous, discipline in every-thing, and commitment are essential.

This book is a great resource. I hope Necessary Confinement becomes a primer for all the readers who are ready to do their work and become better versions of themselves.

Vivia M. Brown

PREFACE

As much as I would love to tell you about the story of my life, this is not the focus here, that will be another book written another day. I want to focus on the transformation and all the tool I found in my toolbox during that transformation that are standard issue to us all. Yes, I meant standard issue, because each of us possess the very simple tools to become and overcome anything placed in front of us. A motherless boy dumped on the streets by an addict father is the ultimate sob story, but I am not here to mope, I am here to tell you how to cope and hope through the hardest journey of your life. That is the journey to YOU.

In 2010, I lost my first and oldest son to the prison system. Shortly before he was incarcerated, he got into some trouble and, immediately after that, I sat down with him and spoke about the principles that I had taught him along the way. I asked him to stay a few days at my house, which was empty - since I traveled a lot - to isolate himself from the friends he was hanging with. I did this because I saw him going down a path I knew wouldn't end well.

I tried to convince him that he was more than just a 20-year-old man with a son and that the things he was subjecting himself to were completely avoidable. He had a choice; I urged him to CONFINE himself to THAT place in his mind, to do the right thing, and to separate himself from his current friends. My hope for him was that he learned how to pull himself away from people because isolation would give him the things needed to identify his true friends and the true meaning of his life.

Consider this: in a lot of our bible readings, there is always a reference to those important men going up into the mountains. Moses went into the mountains and came down with the ten commandments. Jesus went up into the mountains to prepare for the next phase of His journey and to prepare for His death. There are a lot of different reasons why these men went to isolate themselves, but one common theme. That theme is to get closer to the creator in order to gain a better understanding of what He needs from us.

Silence. Having a silent place in your mind is what necessary confinement is all about, in a nutshell. You will never, on a planet with 7.2 billion people, find a place where you can isolate yourself from everyone, unless you find yourself in a Robinson Crusoe or Tom Hank's 'Castaway' type situation. But what you will find is, in instances where people have been in those isolated situations, those individuals have always come back stronger than they ever were. Necessary Confinement is about gaining strength through mental isolation, universal connection with your inner you, and getting the most out of every action you take in life. It's about utilizing your energy, knowledge, and love as tools to transcend into a very good carpenter of life.

I would never be the person I am had I not gone through those moments where I felt most alone. So how do we conquer the loneliness and the isolation? How do we become thoughtful creatures without being on the brink of mental or emotional collapse? We learn to love ourselves for ourselves.

Where this story starts, and where it will end, is in a place of absolute isolation so you can truly see yourself, because the person you see in the mirror will not always be the person looking back at you. It is a much better person, a purer person, and, if I can help to shine a light on that, I know you will become a bigger and better version of yourself. Much like a shadow on the ground at a particular time or an angle aided by the same light at a different time of day. You can always be bigger and better than what you are, and that's the ultimate goal. This book will not be a dry read; it will be very raw. I hope you enjoy it and have a happy reading. See you on the other side…

-*Wes Graves*

CONTENTS

Necessary Confinement

CHAPTER 1

THE NEED TO CONFINE AND REFINE

"You find peace in the confinement of silence."
-Pam Malow-Isham

Like I said in the intro, this is not *that* book; you know, the one where the person professes their unwavering faith and love for God and gives the universe all the credit for their position or outcome in life. Yeah, no! This is a book ten years in the making about how to take the tools you were born with and make yourself the person you know you can be. It's about gaining perspective and pursuing perfection by standing in your strength. I offer you no guarantees that my perspective is the only way to overcome adversity. I do understand that people will criticize, and I invite it - no lie. It is that type of criticism I am going to use to build my continued case; that no-one is perfect, but you can be perfectly you when you know who the hell you are. I admit that my writing style may throw you for a loop every now and again, but be patient and keep an open mind.

Why is confinement necessary? This is the question we need to answer to get everyone focused on this journey of growth, so let's start there. Each inspirational story starts with the horrors of the author's childhood and the obstacles the author had to overcome, and I promise to share those with you every step of the way. I don't need a pity party; I'm built for the shit I had to shovel. What *will* be different about this book is how I share the ways I viewed very complex situations and difficult hurdles. I will confirm and confront the fact that we will all encounter hard ship in life. Lastly, I will try and give you a different way of viewing things that I used to enhance my own self-development. I'm not saying it's perfect, but I do know it works.

For over two decades of my life, I have practiced what I call ego refinement. I don't have a PHD in psychology, so I won't sue if you eggheads decide to use it in the future — just a note for the critics. Ego refinement is the act of self-assessment taken to a very spiritual level. To be good at anything, you have to be aware of everything that is slowing your progress; that is what ego refinement helps you with. The first thing that was required when the journey started was the truth. The truth of who I was and what I wanted to be had to lie within me, so I had to be absolutely honest about everything I was and wanted to be. I was a young father with four kids and I wanted to be a good father more than a great man. That was truth number one. I wanted to be a success but not make a mess of life, that was truth number two. I wanted to be powered by something and not someone seeking power, that was truth number three. Lastly, I wanted everyone who ever poured into me to be proud of what I would ultimately become. None of these were impossible to do, but all of them were met with obstacles. That is why I'm going to share the tricks to running an obstacle-laden race to make the best you.

Necessary Confinement

The first trick to the refinement of your ego is the confinement of the three amigos. See, psychologists always speak of the three: Id, Ego, and Super Ego. I won't try and go all out scholar on you, but we have to briefly cover them. As you may already know, the id part of your conscious self is the softer of the three. This guy or girl is typically the good angel on your shoulder and the conscientious objector of all your stupid missions. The ego part of your conscious self is the person you typically display to the world. This is who your friends call you and who your co-workers know you to be. Your Super ego is 'That Guy,' the one no-one wants to see but is always there, itching to show their ass when someone steps out of line. The little devil on your shoulder.

That is the simple explanation of a very complex thing we all have, but seldom master the refining. The three all have their own name and their own claim on you. One is responsible for your reactions based on experience and data. One is responsible for your safety and response to the environmental. Then, there is the one that has to mitigate and manage the other two. To refine your ego is to understand that they are the essence of you and that your spiritual, mental, and physical selves rely on them to play their roles perfectly. There is a space in your mind that filters noise and a space in your heart that filters feeling. Unfortunately, there is not a way to filter all the bullshit that happens in the various environments you may find yourself in. To do so requires controlling your environment relentlessly or confining yourself. Since the latter is unproductive and kind of weird, learning how to be mentally immune to people's crazy is the key.

That is where the tools of Necessary Confinement come in. Here, you learn how to look at all the various aspects of life and the obstacles within it as training tools teaching you how to navigate on your journey to a better you. We will start by facing the Spiritual aspect of life. Without understanding you, your faith, and your place in the universe, you will generally find yourself floating through life; storms will easily push you where you don't want to be. Whether you believe in God or you are that person who identifies as "A Spiritual Person," you have to start with FAITH.

The Need to Confine and Refine

❖ Have you evaluated your three layers of YOU (Id, Ego, and Super Ego) how do each contribute to your refinement journey?

CHAPTER 2

GOD-GUIDED AND LOVE-LED

"Love yourself unconditionally, just as you love those closest to you despite their faults." -Les Brown

There are tons of people that are pointlessly confined in their owns minds. So, what are your first thoughts when you awake? Mine are those of thanks, then relief, followed by joy - a joy that I have been given another chance to dance. Another chance to be and to do something greater than I was able to do just hours ago, the day before. I get another opportunity to be great! I make the decision that, no matter what happens on this day, I will be the strongest and most influential spirit walking this planet because I will be God-powered, God-guided, and love-led. I will free my thoughts and feed my mind with positivity.

A few things need to be clarified: I say God but, for some, this being is consistently referred to as the Universe. Not a man or a woman, but the whole universe. The quiet. The peace. The constant. If you think of IT that way, you will come to realize that the Universe is Love. It is the expansion and continued growth of something special and life altering, while there is then the fear of its contraction or end. Yeah, I just tied that all together like a monk or some shit -right?

The Universe (GOD) is our guide when it comes to understanding love. The conditions are simple: exist, and I will love you. Violate every rule or law, and I will love you. You will be born imperfect, and I will provide you all the same opportunities, air to breath, and the ability to exist in my love - thus says the Universe. It took me years to realize this simple fact.

The simple existence of a child changes what you know love to be and often embodies what unconditional love feels like. Along with that guidance from our spiritual Creator, we gain love for the love a child represents, and that transforms us forever. How, you might ask? The power of knowing that love is the compass of our conscience. Nothing that is done is without love in it - or hate overtaking the love that once existed - and, from here, we are forever led by love.

Love-led is more about the understanding of where love comes from, and how it exists without conditions, than it is about the drivers behind the emotion. For example: she may be pretty now, but it won't last forever, so love-at-first-sight is sort of lame and I see it simply as lust or love-in-the-light. On the other hand, she's so generous, the condition is added, and it means that she means nothing without something aiding her existence in your life. Adding value to life and if met on the same level, there is a love affair that will make most vomit in their mouths. Real love is love on an endless reel.

That is exactly what a love-led relationship looks like. It's very typical to question everything in love and I give this advice frequently: Before you ask the question about the dirty socks, ask whether he is tired. He may respond with, "why'd you ask", and you say "because you never leave your dirties on the floor baby, and if you are too tired for that, then I want to do something to change that spirit." Bam, that shit wasn't hard at all, was it? For a man that comes home to a dirty house, he is questioning, with love, "how did I leave all this for my wife to do," and he becomes more conscious of his behaviors and his own nastiness. All these changes occur because you are love-led and find joy in showing that there is no condition that will cause you to hate your significant other or allow your love for them to dissipate. While I make it sound easy to be God-guided and love-led, it isn't without some simple principles to follow in order to keep you on the path to perfecting you.

The four principles of perfecting you are spiritual awareness, emotional preparedness, mental declaration, and physical preparation. If practiced, these principles will help to eliminate the love/hate barriers and make decisions that will include logic and love.

All four principles are codependent to live a God-guided and love-led life.

~ **Spiritual Awareness** – connect with God; He is within you. The God inside you will guide you to become the person you are designed to be. Be the best you…

~ **Emotional Preparedness**– strive to attain a higher level of consciousness, don't take anything personal, reach into the universe on a spiritual level, and connect with people as fast as you can. Master loving yourself and others unconditionally, even those who spite you.

~ **Mental Declaration** – foster the mental agility to confront and overcome daily hazards and obstacles with the knowledge that you will persevere. No person goes through life without facing challenges; how you respond and the meaning you assign to the challenge is what will make the difference in your life.

~ **Physical Preparation** – The physical "will" to get out of bed is directly connected to your spiritual, emotional, and mental state.

Remember, love for yourself is the primer for all love that will exist in your life. That includes love for the people you currently love and those in the future that you will come to love.

God-Guided and Love-Led

❖ Think back over your day. What were your very first thoughts and how did they influence the remainder of your day? EX. Mine is "POWER-THROUGH"

CHAPTER 3

DISCIPLINE IN EVERY-THING (DIET)

"An undisciplined life is an insane life." —*Socrates*

In my first two years of High School, I took Latin. Don't judge me. One of the first words to stick out to me was the word Discipulus, meaning knowledge or instruction. It stuck with me and eventually became the focal point of all things in the form of the word Discipline. I won't pretend I am lapse-free of laziness - that would suggest I am no longer human - but I take this part of my life deadly serious. Why? Because everything I want to be requires something more of me and no-one else. That is what knowledge (Discipline) is; the accumulation of experience through life, whether retained for its usefulness or disdained for its abusiveness. Life is a discipline that requires discipline to live it to its fullest.

So, I say the word diet and every group or individual I speak to about it instantly convulses. I smile and then break into this very animated discussion because, for me, it is the most provocative acronym I've ever come up with and it is the code to a "virtual safe" that holds all our potential inside it. While God's guidance and balancing the phases of life are, on and beneath the surface, necessities, you cannot sustain success at the things in life that really matter without applying DIET (Discipline In Every-Thing).

When I left the military, I was always on a different type of diet. I was not a body builder or anything of the sort, I was simply a very conscious person and what I knew about a change in lifestyle (Soldier to Civilian) was that when you leave an environment that demands your physical preparedness, you should probably remain prepared for life. A change in nutrition or lifestyle for weight management and/or health reasons is always good for modifying your trajectory towards where you want to be in life.

The funny thing about the acronym (DIET) and the diabolical word "Discipline" is they both suffer from the scarlet lettering of having a negative connotation, most people despise the derivative and the witticism, but every person admits they need both at or in some phase of their lives. For every purpose imaginable, Discipline serves you well. Its application builds mental, emotional, spiritual, and physical strength regardless of the area applied. You learn to be unapologetic when it comes to your time. You learn to devote "Love Me Time" to your day. You also learn to hold yourself accountable. Everything that I will write about in this book is centered on this single acronym, DIET For myself, the adage "hindsight is 20/20," holds so much truth; most of my failures were due to my lack of discipline. When I corrected this, I changed forever.

True story: one day I was sitting on my couch watching a Law and Order marathon and cutting the grass for five hours in my mind, but never a single blade of grass in reality. The disappointment that I felt when I looked up and saw it was dark outside was not because the neighbor's grass was going to look better on Sunday morning. It was because, for all that I am, I am not a lazy or procrastinating type and I allowed something to slow me down. I allow myself to fail me. I turned the T.V. off and did not watch T.V. again for five years.

I would go to the movies with my kids weekly and buy movies to enjoy with my family at home, but if I went to someone's home and they were watching T.V. then I would leave them to it. I concluded that I should not be squandering my time and allowing these types of distractions to capture my attention. I needed to isolate myself. This one simple act changed my life forever. I was reading everything and anything, I was learning more than I needed to know about my job and other people's jobs. I wanted more knowledge and needed less mess, meaning, (no commercials): you cannot sell a killer whale nail polish.

True discipline exists in our subconscious mind. Subconsciously, we all have a level of discipline that we apply daily without thought, whether it be brushing our teeth, showering, or taking the same daily route to school or work. We do these things without thinking because the repetition eliminates supposition in your outcome or result. If you leave at a certain time, you know you will get to work on time if all things remain the same. When you find the formula (route to take + time to leave = on time) you follow it without question. That is what DIET is all about; taking steps to understand that **Discipline (is required) In Every-Thing** you do. It is about you formulating, on a daily basis, all of the equations that rescue you from a less effective version of you. Applying **Discipline in Every (little or big) Thing** is done by deliberately thinking through your day and saying, "this is a good thing, this is a bad thing," and deciding the good can stay while the bad can go away.

When this becomes second nature to us, our subconscious adopts, adapts, and seamlessly performs the actions we train it to do. My mind is trained to get the list done. When I say I am going to do something, I cannot sleep without the task being accomplished. If I do, it is typically a very short sleep with shallow results as far as rest. There are conscious decisions that we all make daily, i.e., studying to maintain or exceed a certain GPA, seeking opportunities at your job for advancement, training for a marathon, or even changing your diet and adopting a healthy lifestyle. To be successful, this requires our subconscious mind to adopt the task assigned and consciously carry out our decisions without deviation from the (successful) behaviors, essentially making my subconscious mind a Disciple of the conscious commitment.

Remember, it takes 21 days to form a habit and 66 days to develop any skill. Whatever areas in your life you want to improve, apply more deliberateness and Discipline. Make it a Conscious Commitment and Subconscious Conviction! Make it a part of your daily DIET (Food for Thought).

Discipline In Every-Thing (DIET)

❖ Do you apply **DIET** as a way of life? Think about how you spend your day. What are some things you wish to change? Write it down and apply **DIET** consistently for 21 days.

Wes Graves

CHAPTER 4

LOVE, THE CURRENCY OF LIFE

"The human heart is like a ship on a stormy sea driven about by Winds blowing from all four corners of heaven." - Martin Luther King Jr.

The power of love is well documented, always on display, and requires a vast amount of discipline. We talked about DIET in the last chapter and love is not exempted from the long list of things that require the application of Discipline In Every-Thing. The irrational acts of anger and hurt that love causes are demonstrated and chronicled by every person who has experienced heartache. Our children deal with it and it hurts for us to watch them suffer through it. But, have you ever stopped to evaluate that moment when everything was alright again? That moment when recovery ends with the discovery that life is still good, it's just a little less complicated by the responsibility of owing someone 'LOVE'? The death of a relationship

35

with someone else always causes a revitalization of the relationship with 'self.' I always say, love never goes away when the person does; it finds a better way to display itself through 'Self Love.'

I am born into a condition whereby if I love, I shall be loved. If I discern love, I know how valuable it is to me, so I should give it abundantly. I know what it is to live without love, so I choose to be charitable. I know what the absence of love does to me, so I choose to work for it and invest my own for the chance to benefit at least a value reciprocal to that which I invest. This is the very unconscious rationale we adopt from the moment we understand love and this is the moment we become brokers of love. Like all brokers, there is a commitment to profitable efforts and a willingness to accept loss as a result of doing business with the wrong person. You cannot always know whether the person is going to be worth the energy, but you can be sure of your own efforts and commitment to be a good steward of one's heart.

The concept of love as the currency of life struck me one day as I was grieving the loss of someone dear to me. I banged my head over the fact that I may not have shown that person the love that they deserved, and then I went deeper into my memory and tried to quantify the time spent. Not the money spent, but the time spent. I made this person laugh constantly and the few times she was angry with me were worth it. I started to realize that I was a much better person than that person may have thought. I was the dollar you find in the laundry and not the lint in the vent. I then reviewed all of the relationships I had been in and realized much of the same. My love was valued less over time and eventually held no value to the people who once thought it was all they wanted in the world. The value of me didn't decrease; the value of love did and they could not see it anymore.

A hell of a parallel but as true as anything written, love is much like money. Love is an absolute necessity of life, as is money. It is like air; you suffer and die without it. Where it differs is in this way; if money is the root of all evil, love is the root of all life. A cold and unloving heart is miserable and does not truly live. A love-filled heart recognizes joy and transports harmony into the world even when there is no acknowledgement of love towards them. Yep! The value of love ebbs and flows like sea waves and stock prices; its value increases, decreases, or remains constant during different stages of life.

Check this out: imagine a person who is poor. It is conceivable that such a person would find so much value in having wealth. In contrast, someone who is affluent would value wealth differently and may have difficulty comprehending the barriers of those who are less fortunate. The same is true for people who are rich in love. The irony sometimes is that people who are 'love rich' (living a life with everything they love close) may take it for granted, while a person without love (a loner), would do anything and everything to have access to it.

Here is what I want you to walk away with: love is a currency that helps in our social exchanges. If you have love, use it and value it like you would do with real money.

Yep, I am saying be stingy and philanthropic all at the
same time. See, we can love everyone (taxes) and then
there are those that we must love with causality (bills). But
there is a love that belongs solely to you (savings, pension,
and 401K) that you must share sparingly. These three
come with all the hard work you put into developing a life
with a person. The savings are often built early on with the
time spent and love made. The pension is what you take
from the relationship as a lesson from love lost; it lasts a
lifetime. The contribution from the end of the relationship
is what you must cash in on if you plan to make the next
relationship work. If you let it roll over into the next
relationship, you are likely to benefit less than you would
expect because all of the real value is in the accessible truth
and understanding of what went wrong after you invested
all that time. How did my love lose its value?

Understanding love as the currency of life goes
even deeper than as we have addressed to this point. Life
is dependent on inputs and has very little value itself. Love
is an output that increases the value of life based on the

input of love. Without getting too geeky, that means that love can increase its boundaries and make life more, but life doesn't do that by itself or for love. The poor person learns to live with less and embraces the input of new wealth very easily if they win the lottery. That is how love should be valued.

Nothing will prevent you from robbing the metaphorical bank account of the people you love on occasion. But, if you delve into the full understanding of love as the currency of life, it will embolden you to make many deposits with the expectation there will be real returns on your investment in the form of lessons. The return is not merely exclusive to love as it affects the person's total actions; they will become a more inspired person, a better lover, a better friend, mother, father, etc. That is the return on investment I am speaking of in regards to love being the currency of life. This is the expectation I encourage you all to have when you pour your love into someone.

Maya Angelou said, "I've learned that people will forget what **you** said, people will forget what **you** did, but people will never forget how **you made them feel.**" There is a difference between watering a thriving flower bed and watering dead flowers incapable of growth. What I am saying is that you must know when to say when. The most important thing you can do before you cut someone loose or end a relationship is to understand what hand you had in it.

We each personally know at least two of them; people we have given everything to or helped in every way imaginable. I had a person I thought very highly of and considered just as valuable as a family member. When the time came to extinguish the relationship, I continuously revisited the things I had done for them and agonized over the effort wasted. Then it dawned on me that what I had done over all that time was practice investing my love in someone. I had essentially studied a book and from those lessons came all the blessings I needed.

The Revelation: Instead of looking at someone like they were worthless or not worth my time, I had to examine the person I was to them with the understanding that I was either a thumb or a pinky.

To make sense of that, consider the fact that you have three fingers between your thumb and your pinky. As you hold that hand in front of you, palm facing you, you can evaluate the relationship the thumb has with the pinky finger. The thumb is the strongest of the fingers and the pinky is the weakest. When we evaluate our relationships, that is generally what we identify first; the strength or weakness of our position within that relationship. But, consider this: the thumb cannot carry half the load of a pinky because of how it is positioned on your hand. The true value of the relationship is in understanding the value of the love in the relationship. Having that loved-one is like having a perfect stock; you value it for the consistent growth.

Love, The Currency of Life

❖ Evaluate your relationships (personal and professional), how much are you pouring in and what is the profit gained from your investment?

CHAPTER 5

BUILT FOR THE 'BULLSHIT'

"The ultimate measure of a man is not where he stands in moments of comfort and convenience, but where he stands at times of challenge and controversy." -Martin Luther King Jr.

On the upper part of my back, I have a tattoo that I think explains everything about my approach to life. It is my motto, mantra, and fight song: "Built for the Bullshit." I spent years saying it to friends, family, and colleagues, so once I found myself in a horrible mental space, I moved beyond the banter and embraced it. We are built and equipped to handle all of life's trials, though we often think we are not.

My formative years have prepared me to be a skillful matador in this bullpen of life and, as I maneuver, I found myself faced with countless instances of life's **bullshit** hitting me in the face - and the **Bull's hit** shattering my faith. The duality of the word sparked my interest and I found it to be spot-on as a tool to explain the two competing things we are faced with in life. One being the circumstances we find ourselves in because we stepped in the bull shit, and two being the resulting mental injury from the bull's hit.

"The ultimate measure of a man is not where he stands in moments of comfort and convenience, but where he stands at times of challenge and controversy." These powerful words by the infamous Martin Luther King Jr. remind me of this particular event that I consider to be a turning point in my life. I was fresh out of the Army, leaving behind a thing I was passionate about. I walked out into a world that was very unwelcoming and did not see me or any of my accomplishments in the military as something impressive. I had many doors slammed in my face. Through it all, I had to remind myself not to be discouraged. I am built for this and I have endured the worst of things in this short life. The murder of my mother at the age of 7 years old, being abandoned by my father, berated by uncles and men who would be mentors had I chosen to be nothing in life. Through each experience, I leaned heavily on the acquired faith and strength which many would say should not exist in a child who has been shat on by life.

My mother's death wasn't the worst thing that happened to me. Her death actually took me from an environment that could have consumed me or made me a monster and placed me into one where I could possibly thrive. I was taken, by my father, to a world and home that was filled with love and a promise of a bright future, although he would quickly rip that from me and then abandon me. The abandonment of my father made me realize that being a father is more important than fathering a child. It is not a temporary job; it is a lifetime responsibility and requires total commitment. Just because you are able to father a child does not mean you are built for that shit.

The berating from uncles telling me I wouldn't amount to much taught me the psychology of the weak minds of weak men. Most of their generation were drug addicts and failed fathers, so they could not offer me insight on my outcomes in life. I knew that I had to build the tools to endure them because it was clear to me that I was being led by what I considered broken men.

All the struggles proved me strong, yet a couple of days before my 25th birthday I found myself completely overwhelmed during a moment of reflection. What the Universe wanted of me was causing me an emotional crisis that had triggered a mental melding. All of the negativity I had endured that fueled hate in my heart became the mental fuel to overcome the emotional hurdles. In that moment of lamentation, it was as if The Universe answered me itself... Clear as day: "son, there was no way you could have survived it all and be who you are today if I had not prepared you for it..."

Necessary Confinement

I was built to withstand all the bullshit life could deposit on my path. I gave up on all perceived negative influences and, in a loving way, I mentally isolated myself from being a victim in any situation.

Listening to The Universe made me resilient. If you listen closely, you will recognize Her teaching you lessons even through your hurt and pain. We are all built for the Bull's Hit; how quickly you recover from hurt and pain is indicative of your faith, your strength, and your resolve.

Built for the 'Bullshit'

❖ How do you constantly refine your skills to maneuver through life's bull shit? What is your fight song?

CHAPTER 6

GREENER GRASS: THE COLORS IN YOUR GARDEN

"Life is just that easy, and people are just that complicated."
-Wes Graves

Beneath your feet lies the place and space the Universe has set aside for you. You are always where you should be, but you may not always be doing the work you should be doing. That work is growing. Personal Growth. Growing in that space and time. To develop the ability to be confined in a place in your mind where growth is continuous, we cannot be disingenuous. You must be honest with yourself about what you are and where you are in life to go and grow further.

There is not a topic I will address in this book that you haven't heard from the mouths of your favorite aunt or uncle, and I certainly won't veer far from the course of our current social problems, which are simply a repeat of history. I am referencing the loss of our cultural identities and the fact that our children are failing to see the value of the lessons from the previous generations. The generation of kids that grew up during the civil rights movement fell dead into the disco trap. The cocaine and dance life. The generation that grew up as Cosby Kids had to watch their children fall into the 'Trap-Life' trap, which led to the crack and twerk era. Fortunately, we find ourselves at yet another enlightening, and guess what? We should get this shit right if we want our grandkids to survive the next wave of craziness. The threat of the next era of craziness is why we must become aggressive agriculturalists. We must learn to raise the most fruitful generation of children. We must learn to be the perfect gardeners.

It all starts with you. Like most of you, in my early years I found it hard to appreciate the good things about myself. I only saw the things I needed to improve. I was so fixated on correcting the perceived negative things, I did not give myself credit for the great things. 'Chucck' was a great guy and I didn't realize how much I didn't like him.

'Chucck' is the name I went by most of my life. I don't care much for the name because it became a stain on my brain and a haunting influence on my psyche. It always reminded me of my father and his very-imperfect-self. The colors in your garden are representative of the relationship we have with ourselves. The garden you were given by the Universe is yours to mend and attend. Many of us waste so much time weeding, we forget to build the scarecrow to keep out the birds that would have their way with it. We build fences but fail to adequately water our garden. We must be as educated as we want our children to be. We must be as disciplined as we want our children to be. It is really that simple.

My Garden (self) was perfectly grown to the standard by which it was designed; it was up to me to be a master gardener and ensure my garden thrived to its full potential. I was so fortunate that I got to spend four seasons with my Grandmother, just her and myself. I learned so many lessons from her that still I find myself amazed. It was as if she was Mr. Miagi and I was the

Karate Kid. As a child, she taught me that limitations are self-afflicted mental obstacles added to a path the Universe made perfect for you. She would often walk me to her garden to do work. I hated it - the work that is. On one of those occasions, she told me that the most important thing you can learn from (this) a garden is how to work on seeing the beauty in it. If the sweat on your face is not a good indication of something beautiful taking place, the greenery and health of the garden should be more than enough. Take a look at it after the work is done and give thanks that none of the sweat was a waste.

You only need to plant, pray, and prepare a table for the graces of God. I didn't understand it. How could I, at nine-years-old? Honestly, I didn't understand until I was about twenty-five. Her point was, the vegetables I enjoyed in my soup came from a garden you built with your hands. Those vegetables were surrounded by things like weeds and rocks and varmints that may be harmful. However, while they have a greater purpose, that purpose is to keep you focused on your purpose. Don't forget the work, even if it is behind you at this point. That same work must be poured into your children and grandchildren. To enjoy the fruits of life, we must continue to work on the rows and pull the weeds that pop up.

We are dressing our kids to show that the garden is pretty. Their life is good. But, is it? Are they well-read or read to at night? Do they get the undivided attention they cherish? I can tell you that I was a decent father. I lost two sons to the prison system and questioned that reality up until a few years ago, but I feel comfortable saying it and even better letting my children reserve their right to judge me on it. I know that I gave them some strong roots and that their gardens had very few weeds. That is the work I speak of here. You know what it was that plagued your garden growing up. The rocks and the weeds. The drugs and alcohol abuse in the household that created doubt, fear, and shame in your child's mind. The disparate friends that created chaos in your family circle. I call these weeds because they impede your family's ability to grow close and remain solid. Keep the pressure and emphasis on education, because the light they need to grow is in a book, not on television. This is the work, the mending and attending you must do to make sure that their gardens are as good as they can be when you hand them over to them.

You are perfectly YOU. Remember this. Our uniqueness makes us different from our peers. Where we get stuck is not recognizing the link between self-worth and self-awareness. Being self-aware doesn't necessarily mean we understand our value, and understanding our value doesn't mean we are self-aware. The weeds don't make the garden worthless, they make the work necessary. To be the best version of yourself, possessing the qualities of self-awareness and self-worth, are a must. Self-awareness is found in identifying the weeds to increase your growth and development, becoming a better version of yourself, building your self-worth, embracing the beauty of your garden, and accepting and loving yourself regardless of your weeds.

Reflect on your hard work, but don't gloat. Acknowledge your efforts and take a bow. It is you that is responsible for the beautiful, colorful, flourishing flowers in your garden, so love all of them.

Greener Grass: The Colors in Your Garden

❖ As the sole landscaper, how much work are you investing to improve the quality of your garden?

CHAPTER 7

THE PHASES OF LIFE: THE MULE, MUSTANG AND STALLION

"If you're walking down the right path and you're willing to keep walking, eventually you'll make progress." -Barack Obama

Do not choose your path with hesitance; walk it with passion, walk it with vigor, and then gracefully bow-out. If we are lucky, we get to take a bow for a job well done. I work tirelessly to be the best me, or what I today refer to as a Stallion. That is what the Mule, Mustang, and Stallion allegory is all about. We all share the common temptation at one point or another to quit because, in life, there is some heavy lifting. I often write or speak to people about the different phases of life; this is the most critical of things for us all to understand about our state of being. Our very short existence here on earth is all about the blazing of paths and the hoofing required to enjoy the trip. As we hump through life with the weight of the world on our backs, it helps to understand that we are performing based on the phase of life we are operating in.

You are either operating in your Mule Phase, your Mustang Phase, or your Stallion Phase. While I say Stallion, consider that this is a gender-neutral analogy and I am not saying that, as a woman, this doesn't apply to you. Women, just like men, are stallions when they reach the phase in their life where they know their full value and walk in that power. To briefly clarify the three titles prefixed to the phases, consider these animals and their attitudes. Consider how we used them all, both now and in the past. The mule is a very docile creature, often seen as a slow or dumb and only useful for carrying loads, hard work, and plowing. A mustang is almost always seen as a strong-willed creature that bucks for the sake of its freedom and independent existence. A mustang does not go through the breaking process easily, and neither do we humans. They are often used in a circus fashion or rodeo to amuse us. The stallion is graceful and genteel; it carries itself majestically because it is treated that way. They are used for racing and breeding for equestrian shows. We all have these three attributes within us. I will try my best to paint the picture of how they exist within us and why it is important to recognize the phase you are in. If you recognize it, I promise you will quickly make the adjustments to advance yourself to the best version of YOU.

The various phases of life can be a simple picture to draw and I will try to illustrate them here as best I can. Consider, as young adults our friends have a major amount of input into what we think, do, and where we head on our path in life. Most of the load and stress on us in this phase is caused by peer pressure and low referencing tools or knowledge. Our friends are smarter and we don't know why, so we follow them - or we are all dumb as hell and where we end up doesn't matter, so you follow any way. Slowly, we all start to form our own opinions and agendas and, before long, choose our own path in life. We use small inputs to steer our friends toward our agenda and, when they waver or refuse to go in that direction, we ditch them to follow that which is more important to us. When I say ditch them, I don't mean stop loving them; I simply mean we leave them at that fork in the road. We lose friends and relationships we value at the change of each phase; embracing that fact is what this chapter attempts to cover.

We all have the experience of being either a mule, a mustang, and/or a stallion during this wild race through life. In your younger adult years, you are constantly working to understand the goals and meaning of things that bring you very little satisfaction. You are generally being whipped into shape for what society needs you to do. Generally, you are not focused on much outside the field (of work) you are plowing away at. Slowly and methodically, you plug away at a task that requires no real thought. This does not mean you have no great aspirations or things that you want to do to impact the world, it just means that you have settled into your role in society. It means that the world has found you before YOU found you; that you were given a job to do without considering the work meant for you. It is the realization of this that brings out the rebel inside in the form of the mustang. The bucking begins from the growth within. The confined and refined version will always make its way to the surface.

Now, the Mustang phase of life is a very tumultuous one and honestly anything can happen during this phase. This is the phase of adulthood where divorces peak and children are left with grandmothers for whole decades. This is the phase where men think of themselves more - and in this generation, I think women do too. The phase where women are afraid of being dependent on a man because the men in their lives are as interchangeable as the pantyhose that they may choose for their Sunday morning church dress. It is a wild phase where little is accomplished as far as success, but a lot of life is lived by the person going through this phase. This is also the longest phase of life, ranging from 17 to about 31 - God help our souls, right?

The Mustang phase of life is the hardest phase to get over if enough mistakes are made during the phase. Even as I write this, I feel the twinge of regret surfacing, as I was a 'Mother-Bucker' during my Mustang Phase. I made every mistake twice and missed more opportunities to be a better person than I have time left to make up for. I was always a thoughtful person; I just didn't think much during this phase. Along the way though I saw something in my children's eyes that opened my eyes. In the back of those loving eyes, they saw the Stallion I wasn't even close to being. My children saw me, they revered me, and I owed it to them and all the other people who lift me up in their eyes to be that version of myself.

The Stallion phase is where all the real work is done. You go through the shoeing process - the encasing of your hoofs or feet - essentially preparing for your true path, learning to watch your step, and pick your battles. To get real mileage out of this life, you must accept this as a desired undertaking. When you reach this phase, you carry yourself in a majestic manner so that the true mission and purpose of your life is achieved. You accept your role in the barn (the world) so that you can reach and teach the people you find most important. During the transition to this phase, you spend a lot of time apologizing and rebuilding bridges you have destroyed, but jumping less fences and kicking less barn walls due to frustration. You may never need the relationship again, but you need to know that what was left in the wake of that reckless phase is better than how you originally left it. It purifies the soul and simultaneously empties the trash can in your mind, allowing you to add to both again. It allows you to build that sacred space in your mind that confinement requires for refinement to occur.

The Stallion phase is the phase where your job is now a career and, even if you've never seen it as such in the previous years, that's what it is now. Your company, your family, and your friends get the best of you and the most out of you. You don't mind admitting that you are better this way. You accept the fact that looking like the fool now is cool, and being the bore you have become helps you more than it hurts you.

Becoming a Stallion or a reasonable adult doesn't mean losing sight of your dreams. We all know of a person who lost sight of their purpose and made a conscious decision to settle in life. It breaks our hearts to hear them reminisce about those goals and dreams. Whether it be settling for a career path, relationship path, or so on, losing sight of your true path is a result of not knowing what phase of life you are in.

At first glance, mules, mustangs, and stallions appear similar, yet these animals are very much different. That is how the phases of our lives are. As we go through the different phases, there may be big transitions or subtle ones. Embrace them all and keep going down the right path.

Experience taught me the plans we designed for ourselves do not always align with The Universe's (GOD's) plan for us. Life also taught me that lack of faith in ourselves will prevent us from rising to our full potential. There are those of us that get stuck in the Mustang Phase because we believe the system is against us and there is no way out except bucking and kicking the shit out of people and/or the system itself. What I encourage you to do here is challenge yourself to hurriedly progress through each of the phases of life. Reflect on the last phase with truth and purpose. Acknowledge your growth and own your story of redemption. Become the Stallion you are destined to be.

The Phases of Life: Mule, Mustang and Stallion

❖ What must you do to graduate to the next phase in life? Write it down.

CHAPTER 8

YOU CAN'T SEE – A FOREST FOR THE TREE

There is a difference between a flower bed and a Garden. One is for show, and one helps us grow-either way both will have you hoeing.
-Wes Graves

My idea of confinement, as well as the need for it, is broader and more difficult to understand without first understanding that the space where we confine ourselves is the same space where we find ourselves. The second leg to this is that we cannot find ourselves without seeing what it is that we want to be. I often say, we are all the same tree in a forest full of fools. Until you recognize the person you want to be most like, you will be a shrub of a man.

In all that I write, my goal is for the reader to progress in their depth of thinking. I often elaborate on previous writings because there are real levels to purposeful development. To give a bit more clarity, in most of my writing I attempt to use the common clichés we use or hear every day. With a slight twist to the title and a curve ball or two, I try to offer new perspective. In my use of A Forest for the Tree, it is simply about understanding your purpose and knowing where you want to grow. It's not just about how you see the future, but how to plan it – Plant it – and make it benefit not only you, but also the Planet.

For many, we aspire to live a life filled with success, but for this to be possible we must be deliberate in choosing the proper 'Forest'. It must be conducive to us thriving and becoming that beautiful tree we wish to be within an illustrious forest. When we understand that, the only impact that matters is the impact that changes all the lives around you. Honestly, that is when a tree adds to the forest.

Positioning yourself in the right forest will allow you access to mentors; that is the overarching theme here. There are so many people who have successfully overcome the same obstacles and most of them want to lend a helping hand. As much as we admire beautiful trees, we know they didn't suddenly appear that way; there is a progressive process involved that allows them to grow strong and achieve their majestic peak. They must survive the same fires and termites of life as the next tree. Choosing the right forest means knowing your purpose and understanding your environment. Where is the best place for you to grow and thrive? "Do I change companies, or do I stay at this company and accept the mentorship offered?" These are vital questions that you must ask yourself. These simple questions are the ones which will determine whether or not you will be successful. Mentorship is important and should be sought for both personal and professional growth and self-development. For men, this may be very hard to do, but it is a significant first step.

Mentorship comes in many flavors and finding the right mentor is not always easy. A few things you should seek and consider when choosing a mentor are as follows:

- There must be a rapport between the mentor and mentee. This is a unique relationship and this connection is a must for the relationship's success.
- The relationship between the mentor and mentee should be a reciprocal one. Mentor and mentee should be open to learning from each other. No-one is above learning.
- The right mentor for you is equipped and knowledgeable with the experience you seek. They have already survived the fires and termites and should be pretty much an expert in navigating the rules from a simple playbook.
- The right mentor is not all-knowing but offers hard truths, builds your self-awareness, and is selflessly committed to your best interests.
- The right mentor will manage your expectations as success is almost never instant, but with persistent and deliberate effort it (success) is eventual.

Much like the small oak tree that receives little light in the shadows of all the great oaks, you will grow at the pace of his grace and be as great as all the other trees if you are where you are supposed to be.

The biggest message in this chapter is the value of having a mentor, regardless of your age and where you are in life. Most are being mentored by good or bad influencers and are oblivious to it. That person you consistently go to for advice? They're a mentor. By consistently seeking them out, clearly their opinions are valued.

Most will argue they don't need mentorship. I used to be one of those people and today I admit to you I was WRONG. We all need mentorship and you are no different. I promise you, all successful people currently have or have had mentors in the past. I learned things the hard way although, over time, I finally figured it out. Life would have been so much easier if I had accepted the advice of others or chosen to learn from their mishaps. I now have a few mentors to assist me as I navigate through my personal and professional endeavors. I got tired of paying for my lessons and missing my blessings. Mentorship armed me with the proper tools and helped to weaponize my knowledge. Mentors helped to prevent me from repeating mistakes.

Being a mentee or mentor is not a promise of an easy road - the work is still required. Think about it, if achieving success was easy then everyone would have it. Countless stories and statistics in the world tell us that if you wish to be exceptional, no matter the job, hard work and discipline are the critical ingredients. Choosing the right forest (environment) for your tree (you) is the first step in goal orientation and will open doors for you and grant you access to those who have been there and survived with the battle scars as proof.

I must beat this dead horse: remember, the key to growth and success is to always surround yourself with knowledgeable people (rich soil). To ensure you grow at the fastest rate you can, nurture your mind, body, and soul. Learn from the experts who are willing to groom you (accept the heat and nutrients of the sun) to be a better version of them, which should amount to the best version of yourself. Always, always be invested in how you care for and develop your roots, so that you too will one day pay it forward and pass along the fruit of all that you and your mentor have labored to achieve.

You Can't See – A Forest for the Tree

❖ **What is your purpose, what is your plan to bring it to life? Write it down.**

CHAPTER 9

WE OVERCOME WITH REAL KNOWLEDGE (WORK)

"Making a mistake in life means that you must WORK twice as hard to make things right, so you should condition yourself for real work by acquiring real Knowledge." —Wes Graves

The best YOU require an annual review of *what* you have achieved, *where* you are in life, *why* you have not achieved the goals you have set, and *who* is in the way of that which you want to achieve. I don't use the *when* because the time is not as important now that it is behind you. What is important about when, is when you notice you are failing – that's what the reflecting should sort out. That's where the **WORK** is, asking the questions that give us the knowledge and know-how to make the adjustment.

No matter who you are, at the close of each year we examine and take inventory of all we have accomplished and reflect on the missed opportunities. We often reflect on what went well and what went not-so-well, making promises to redeem ourselves before the close of the next 365 days. We make the usual New Year's resolutions that we seldom stick to. During those periods of your much-needed mental confinement, it is beneficial for you to look at yourself not just in the mirror in your cells (Place/Space of Peaceful Growth), but at the shadow of yourself. The shadow never makes a mistake because the light used to create it is based on how you stand, WORK, and play in the light. The mistakes we make in life commonly have something to do with our failure to respect the shadow we are making with the mistakes.

Making mistakes in life means that you must WORK twice as hard to make things right. For you to make up the lost ground in a literal 'rat race,' you must condition yourself. I, like you, have made all of the same mistakes, I am sure. Taking things personally at a job and leaving it, only to realize the people didn't know my capabilities because I didn't care to show them, or ending a friendship or relationship based on some rumor versus confronting the issue. My hope is that it is understood that we are all built for the work required to overcome our mistakes, no matter the size or severity.

We Overcome with Real Knowledge (WORK) is a concept I adopted over a decade ago after reflecting on my mentors' teachings over the span of my life. The core of WORK is the fundamental understanding that what you learn throughout life is designed to assist and stretch your growth. There is an opportunity for us all to grow through what we go through. I am not a big fan of clichés, but this one is most appropriate to the message.

WORK originated from the teachings of my grandmother, who I would come to understand as being the first of my many mentors. In her own way, she developed an echo chamber in my mind that was all about work; the sun-up to sun-down type of work she and her generation knew growing up. Her continuous lecturing to me was regarding the importance of being the hardest worker. Her telling me never to let another man outwork me still resonates in my mind to this day. I am certain you had heard that advice before from someone but shunned it, not realizing the missed opportunity. That person could very well have been your mentor-to-be and, whether or not you rejected them, they were there waiting on you to do the WORK

My Grandmother's teachings led to many of the ideologies I espouse and what you have read in this book, like Discipline in Every Thing and the Four Principles of Perfect Living. All of these require doing WORK It would take me two and a half decades to realize the gravity of my grandmother's teachings and the importance of what it was to me. I realize that I only overcame the odds and difficulties in life because I was given life-changing bits of knowledge.

So many of us are oblivious to the wealth of knowledge that surrounds us. If you listen, you will learn at least one thing of value each day regardless of where you are and who surrounds you. There will always be opportunities for growth in all things, good and bad. I encourage you to recognize and take advantage of each opportunity to learn. Recognizing those opportunities is often where the challenge lies. For WORK to work, there must be an understanding that overcoming is strictly at the mercy of your understanding and whether or not a value is assigned to the knowledge being presented in that time and space. Understanding where you fall short and need improvements is important to begin the work in WORK. Reflection is a key piece of learning from our mistakes. Sometimes, we go back in our minds, revisiting what we did or did not think went well, or considering how we could have approached it better to achieve a more desirable outcome.

If you find yourself in a situation where things went horribly wrong and reflection doesn't assist you in understanding the why, I recommend calmly revisiting the conversation with the person in an effort to clearly understand where the communication breakdown occurred. It's true that we learn best from our mistakes and reflection helps to gain a deeper understanding. If you understand why it happened, you will have the necessary information to discern whether a different action would produce a different result. The work is in understanding the outcome so that you KNOW that you grew from it. Reflection is critical to learning from past events; understanding where we went wrong or could go wrong is all representative of the 'real knowledge' to be gained. We are the total sum of our experiences. Though we are all different, much of what we experience isn't new. It's new to us, but someone has already learned the lesson. "A smart man learns from his mistakes, but a wise man learns from the mistakes of others," I'm not sure where I heard this, but I wholeheartedly endorse it. I have grown and learned so much from my experiences and that of others. We have the potential to overcome all things through borrowed and learned lessons. Once we take the time to understand where we went wrong and take the actions necessary for correction, we have done the WORK

We Overcome with Real Knowledge (WORK)

❖ Do you take time to reflect on your day or after significant events (positive and negative); what are the results of your reflection? Do you find that you can almost always find a different approach?

CHAPTER 10

THE POWER IN KNOWING AND NO

"The most powerful bit of advice I can give you is "Know, and No" Know that no one needs your money more than you and No is not a hateful word- it is a shield for the sober soul." –Wes Graves

No, out of the mouth of a certain person, often seems like a vile word. Despite its small stature in our lexicon, no as a simple phrase adds strength to the user's voice, regardless of the volume. I know you have had the experience of a friend asking you for a loan or your child asking for money to do or buy something they deemed an absolute necessity. Often-times, even when I was more than willing to say yes, I would say no to practice the act and to see their response. Oh yes! In both cases, I would say no initially because no is one of the hardest things to say to someone you love and adore. The Grave Mistake many of us make is not knowing when no should be the final answer.

No is a single syllable word that causes the sensation of liberation, when you think about it, yet it brings struggles to many. Literally one of the first words we learn as a child is 'no'; the typical adult response is, "don't say that, that's not a nice word." Then, less than a decade later, they have to teach the opposite and add NO-NO-Squares and all that shish to the child's lexicon. From the very beginning, we are inadvertently taught that no = bad/negative. Which, in turn, potentially materializes into, "I won't ask because I don't want to be told no." Ever heard this before?

Yes, is a perfectly good response - and so is no. Whichever end of the spectrum you are on, either receiver or giver, no is a response. A complete response, at that. I know so many people who struggle with saying no as well as those that struggle with hearing it. I will say this bluntly… know that no is an absolutely great answer, if yes is not an easy one.

What I mean by, 'if yes is not an easy answer' is this: When the proposal or request requires you to neglect something on your list of things to get accomplished, no should be the perfect answer because yes will cause a mess. If you find time or can devise a plan after the conversation, then you can change the answer, but let no come out as smoothly as the yes would until you know that yes won't cause you real stress.

We have heard countless stories of loans given and the loaner never getting repaid. I am talking about money they didn't have to begin with - needed for bills, or even for emergency purposes - and the loaner had an expectation that they would get the money back. Another example is individuals inconveniencing themselves for others, giving their bill or vacation money to someone who is living their best life. I live by a very simple philosophy: No-one needs my money more than I do - if they did, they would have my job and work as hard at it as I do. I have no problem lending money and I love to contribute to the lives and betterment of people; I just won't lend what I don't plan to spend.

My grave mistake is the liberating feeling and strength drawn from me knowing the power in no. Learning how to say, "hell no" at times, "no, thank you" at others, and using whichever variation of no that fits the narrative. This allowed me to manage my priorities and create healthy boundaries.

My message here is simple: if you are a people pleaser, I know 'no' (pun intended) is used sparingly. However, a response of no shows strength and maturity. "Though I value my relationship with you, I am not allowing this relationship to influence me in a decision I am not prepared to commit to." Trust me, I know it isn't that simple, but practice no first in this way": "I am going to have to say no, but I will revisit it after this and, if yes is put in my heart, that's where we will start when I call you back." This is how you come to know the power in no. In most cases, if this is a person in your circle, the person will reflect and so will you. They will come back to the table with a better understanding and acceptance of your response.

The Power in Knowing and No

❖ Do you have a difficult time with 'no'? Think of several scenarios you may encounter and practice your 'no' response with love.

CHAPTER 11

IN CASE YOU MISSED THE POINT

"Trying to define yourself is like trying to bite your own teeth."
-Alan Watts

"I am stuck in my ways... I can't lose weight because it's in my genes... I've been this way my entire life, I'm good, I don't need to do anything different, and this is how God made me." Of course, this is the rhetorical pre-manifestation of a common person's failure to yield results. The raw truth is that all humans are inherently lazy and, without realizing it, we make agreements with our conscious selves without committing them to our subconscious selves. Yes, these are different, and yes, they both require WORK on a mental and emotional level, which is why we miss the point.

I'll be honest, it took me a long time to get here. To realize that hard work and discipline is a necessary

89

conscious and subconscious cabling that must take place for a man to wake up and become successful; to realize that, that man has to WORK his ass off probably 16-18 hours a day, something many of us are unwilling to do. It took me years to realize that, unless we commit ourselves to success on the subconscious level and execute the committal actions on a conscious level, success is left to chance. Why take the chance of leaving it (success) to chance?

I was reading a book the other day and my eyes struck something that I thought was so profound. Through the reading, I was astounded by the fact that though people admire professional athletes as much as they do. Most think they are overpaid and I wondered why. Is it because we can't see the hours of training and study they have invested, the trauma to their bodies from these games, the sacrifices made, and all the requirements they may have that we know nothing of? We see the player on the court or the field doing their thing. Then, off the court and field, we see pictures of their big houses and fancy cars... but, as we often do, we miss the point that by the time we see them on the screen/court/field, we only see the *results* of the WORK and the discipline that they pour into themselves. They know, as we do, that the minute they fail to produce results, they are gone from those teams... Yeah, there's no secret in the recipe for success, but there are 2 KEY ingredients; DISCIPLINE and WORK.

The point should never be missed: NOTHING CHANGES UNTIL WE DO. I was deliberate in making this short as a reminder to us all that the key here is not giving up, to face the truth, and commit to the change you seek. The truth we ignore is that, without discipline and work, you will never achieve any goal.

In Case You Missed the Point

❖ Now that you have implemented Necessary Confinement, have you identified areas to improve on? Write them down, apply DIET and do the WORK.

CHAPTER 12

COMMITMENT IN REFINEMENT

"The game of life is funny, but it isn't a joke, if you are playing make sure it's to win" —Wes Graves

The last eleven chapters addressed several different techniques and strategies to assist with confining yourselves in the same space where we always find ourselves: our minds. The mind is very powerful and the place where our thoughts are born. Everything, good and bad, begins in the mind. It is a sacred space which should be valued and protected from our fleeting beliefs and fears. I cannot stress enough the importance of discipline and doing the work. Continuous refinement requires work, work, and more work. The work is continuous; the depth and breadth of your growth will be indicative of the actions you take, not the tools you find here or in any other book. Also, your growth will depend on your circle and the work you invest together.

To achieve change, it will take deliberate action. It is not an easy process and, I will admit, there are times I fall short, but I acknowledge them instantly and get right back at it - the grind. I evaluate where I went wrong and double my work to get back the ground I lose when I make those grave mistakes. We won't always get it right, but what we can't do is quit. Don't beat yourself up: we're humans. Always remember that tomorrow is a new day and you get another chance to be a better YOU.

I have this saying I encourage others to adopt: "you don't get to judge my great, your job is to love or hate." Meaning, you have no idea of the roads I have had traveled to become this person I am, so you don't get to define who you think I should be. I share the story of conquering my first marathon when I speak at forums because it took a lot of sweat and determination. When I started the training journey, I got knocked back quite a few times by naysayers. I even questioned myself on some of those long, lonely runs. Imagine if I had let that get in the way of my pursuit? I was so glad that I didn't. When I was done running the race, I promised myself never to share my aspirations, but just my completions and celebrations.

How many times have you tried to pursue a goal and had someone try to convince you it wasn't either conceivable or achievable? I have been there a time or two. Doing the work, worked. Coupled with doing the work, I encourage you to always be honest with yourself. When we are not honest with ourselves, we regress and our growth declines. We then fall into this illusion which creates a numbing effect, making us oblivious to the actual truth and, much like having a bad tooth, the truth can linger painfully. There is no such thing as a well-meant lie and that tooth that requires removal or filling will abscess without your attention. Own your truth and grow through your experience. Growth is a lifelong process - a 'climb,' as I like to call it – and it ends only when we cease to exist. Until then, we should continue the practice of self-confinement and see the value of that confinement in our refinement. Necessary Confinement is about that space and place in our mind that allows our growth to be a peaceful undertaking. Mentally induced Self-Confinement is essential to our progression as we continue our journey to become greater versions of ourselves. Ralph Waldo Emerson said, "A great man is always willing to be little." That is why that small cell which you must retreat to will allow you to become the greatest version of you.

Commitment in Refinement

❖ Set SMART (specific, measurable, achievable, realistic and time-bound) goals. Document your progress and stay the course.

Congratulations, you finished the book! The real work now begins. You now have the tools to begin your journey of necessary confinement paving the road to a better you. Thank you for reading and allowing me to share what I have learned with you.

-Wes Graves

Visit Wes Graves

www.nogravemistakes.org

Connect with Wes Graves

Facebook: nogravemistakes.org@growthspirt

Necessary Confinement